The Bone Staircase

Kerry Priest studied Anthropology and Linguistics at Edinburgh University and taught English and Cultural Studies at Eichstaett and Humboldt Universities in Germany. She was one of Eyewear's Best New British And Irish Poets 2018 and has published work in *Poetry Salzburg Review, French Literary Review, Acumen* and in the Emma Press *Future Poems* anthology. She has been shortlisted for the Bridport Prize twice, longlisted in the National Poetry Competition and was nominated for the Forward Prize for Best Individual poem in 2019. She presents a weekly show on Soundart Radio.

Acknowledgements

Some of these poems have appeared elsewhere, and I thank the relevant editors for supporting my work:

'Medicine Wheel' was published in *Acumen*. 'Womb' appeared in *Anything That Can Happen: Poems about the Future* (Emma Press) and in *Dark Mountain*. 'Song of Alice through the Embryoscope', 'Belly', and 'Skin' were commissioned by Mothers Who Make for the Hidden Motherhood project.

I thank Andy Brown for his mentoring; Ros Barber, Hannah Linden, Sarah Acton, Rosie O'Cain and Linsey Fryatt for providing feedback on some of these poems; Jackie Juno and Jodi Feist for their ancestral inspiration; Julie Mullen, Dan Leahy, Susan Taylor and Jennie Osborne for supporting my 'crazy bone lady' phase; Simon Armitage, for suggesting I put a pamphlet together; Rosie Ford, Jack Astor, Karen Murdarasi, Alice Nightingale and Isobel Shirlaw for their help and encouragement; and my husband Stephen for his keen eye.

Contents

for Stephen and Astrid

Prologue

Ancestry

Uncanny stone,
tree as bone,
sediment-nub
from the longwall
of all that's gone.

Nightfall, December,
unscrubbed brick
of a northern town,
the neighbour's cat
curled at a fender.

Old-fangled empire's
Nobodaddy,
you tarred *the road
to nowhere fast*
with your fleeing ire.

In the glossy grin
across your flank,
trees creep,
and insects tick
beneath a trapped sun

waiting to suffer
a second death.
Know this:
even good power
corrupts, Lucifer.

Sulphur fire
for a sweating world,
fistful of smog,
my hands are unclean
as I build your cairn and pyre.

A brass fanfare shrieks
as you commit sati
for my ancestors.
The black seam
inside me creaks.

Round 1 – Biology

When the Doctor Talks about My 'IVF Journey'

You are thirty seven.
Your point of departure
is not the North Pole
but 45 degrees longitude,
just east of Archangel.

It is not too late.
We will catch you
during the two short months
of summer, guide you
over the snow fields

that creak like bones
underfoot, where melting
snow shuffles off the pines,
their needles waxy
against the wind.

We will guide you
south to the taiga,
away from the permafrost,
to that band of green
below the indigo
Baltic. Do you see?

The aspens and willows
are teeming there
with ermine, sable,
queen wasp and butterfly.
I can help you.
There is still time.

Over and Over

How many quads of eyes have watched
her flipchart show of embryos today?

How hesitantly did the couples spear
the plastic practice tummy with a syringe?

Bees gulp at rows of foxgloves in the garden.
Cottonwood seeds eddy past porters heaving trolleys.

Patients check their phones in clouds of cottonwood fluff.
The garden is ice-age deep with the stuff.

And here's how whiteness travels
through summer's scattering of flowers:

wind-scooped seed heads teeter, swerve, then pool
unplanned in lay-bys and by-ways, central reservations.

The cottonwood has evolved to give out so much seed,
but not many of its umbrellas ever make a tree.

The nurse explains the procedure over and over.
Perhaps some of this will stick.

The Killing Moon Has Come Too Soon

As if to prove they're getting old,
it's 80's hour on the waiting room radio.
Let's do the Time Warp again,
let's do the Time Warp again.

Piggy reads Pinky her zodiac.
They lock index fingers across the table.
Don't stop believin',
hold onto the feelin'.

Snubnose wonders if Redcheek's erectile problems
are blood-pressure-related.
I need a cool rider,
a cool rider.

Moustachio fiddles with the radio.
His problem is music's better than sex.
Gotta have House music all night long,
with that House music you can't go wrong.

The Geeks are definitely in love.
Their lopsided smiles curve in unison.
Tell it to my heart,
tell me I'm the only one.

Marilyn Monroe scrolls the newsfeed.
Her insides are cobwebby.
She's got Greta Garbo's stand-off sighs,
she's got Bette Davis eyes.

Snubnose scratches Baldy's head.
Today is their first extraction.
Once upon a time I was falling in love,
now I'm only falling apart.

Extraction

She's on her back
sucking gas and air.

The fallopian probe
sucks out ten eggs
and the nurse scuttles away

like a midwife toad,
the toad who twines
a bunch of eggs
round the back
of his legs

and lopes off in jerks
towards the water.

Song of the Silvery Embryo

Listen when this mirror speaks,
for captured in my complex
are the multitudes I keep.

Oaks whose gnarlings weave in Celtic knots,
the farmers' year measured on a stick,
notch by notch.

Many doors opened, even more closed,
I've seen quick money, slow regret,
big news and no shows.

Focus as my crystal shape unfolds,
for captured in this complex
are the stories of my bones

and I have lived a thousand girls since Eve,
but again and again
you'd better believe,

there's been this one thing:
the sting
of love.

Lines

Bonsai and rocks frame
a pool of pea-gravel.

The Japanese do not say
'Zen garden'
but 'dry mountain river'.

Raked lines suggest the
movement of water

or the lay of well-mucked fields
after the harrowing,
where heavy oxen have been.

Another translation
is 'rotten mountain river'.

The gardener combs and combs.
He ploughs the stones
that will yield nothing.

Round 2 – Astronomy

SpermComet™

The SpermComet™ results are in the mail.
SpermComet. Doctors hunched
over star charts, trace the path
of sperms that zip in flight.

The germ of life on our blue rock
came from a meteorite.
Primal matter, amino acids and complex carbons
hitch-hiked on a comet-seed,
were posted through the atmosphere
and, given water, time and light,
they made a mind that in days gone by
would watch the shooting stars for news.

But now we stand in dressing gowns,
await the second post that never comes,
and last night's shooting stars were nothing more
than asterisks that marked a wish.
They herald no news. No news.

Sparks

He strikes a match and holds it to paper.
A flame catches, scuttles like a panicked mouse.
Blackened edges bleed orange, then falter.

What's the deal with this house?
Is everything filmy, coated in damp?
Why can't the chimney draw?

From the cupboard, he sources a fire-lighter: *Champs,*
but it won't take. Soon he's scorched
his thumb with a match.

Everyone else manages this.
Look at them, smug and hygge in their rooms,
they sit and toast marshmallows, then... squish.

They ladle stove top dollops of soup,
dry their kids' pants, warmed for school,
hang socks and towels, cheeks aglow.

Other families, through fitness or fool's
luck have tapped a channel into the flow.

O, how life's energy breathes
for these normal suburban deities.

Song of Alice through the Embryoscope

Behold the primordial pea.
Alchemists called me *Shamayim,*
a silvery world machine.

Not much to look at, I agree
but I'm dense with sense,
unshakeable as a dream.

~

Already,
I predict a life to come,
             all
                  those
                      trails
                          that
                              will
                                  lead
                                      back
                                            to this

singularity,

this point of expansion.
~
I am giddy with freedom.
I must be human already.

My first choice, though,
is the big one.

~

Dead/alive,
What am I?
       -Schroedinger's dot.

All you've got.

~

Please, don't call me the ouroboros.
I'm far too tiny and too porous.

Besides, I'm growing,
            paring
                      ~ flowering

                    into a double
                              bubble.

            ~

W
h
e
e
e
e
!

~ on day three
                  I dive
                    into the vortex *change.*

I am a chaos of waters, stirred white

~

then I shrink to nothing.

No.

      Not nothing.

Nearly nothing.

~

Almost unmanifest,

I zip down meaty tubes

to behind the prism walls,

the sudden architecture of my body

crystallizing into a palace.

The embryologist

calls me Blastocyst.

I will be a baby.

Or a very
near
miss.

Shooting Star

A white line
streaks across the screen.
It is tiny,
but flashes deep with fire.

Elegy for a Nothing that Never Was

Should she sing for a star that span for a while in the dark,
a shivering and translucent seed,
little more than a trick of light,
a bean that jumped for a day,
a speck of hope,
her little almost,
a thought,
a mayfly,
a dot
?

Gilt

The eagle-shaped brows of Australopithecus,
the sink-hole eyes of Homo Erectus and Homo Habilis
glower at her from their glass caves.

We've watched continents divide,
collapse.

And in the Celtic and Northern Europe room,
there's a gilt gift from the dark ages,
a golden torque, embossed with corded braid-work,
woven through with the painstaking weft of craft,
the strands gathering
to an almost perfect circle.

We've done it in beds and on beaches,
pushed out wet babies in huts, in woods,
all for you, all for you.

And she's wearing it now. Intricate, but leaden,
the handiwork of generations is at her throat.

The millstone tightens around her neck,
compresses nape-flesh, Adam's apple.
A thousand hands on her shoulder
deaden the nerves at the collarbone.
Is this it, then? Is this the end?

Expectation has many faces
in the anthropology museum.

We've come so far together,
memory as DNA,
memory as bone staircase.

Skin

Tonight she overhears her heart pulse
in the kitchen, a polyrhythm to the clock's
interminable stalking of the sleeping sun.

The regalia are waiting: syringe, hormone, wet wipe.
At nine pm precisely, she holds up the syringe
to the light, draws 250 ml from the vial.

The skin of a drum
summons the animal
it is made from.

Some know how to make a drum,
stretch soaked deer skin
over a bent rose willow frame
spend two nights in a trance
where the white and red rivers meet.

She does not know this.
Here's how she burrows between the worlds:

Pinch some tummy chub, pierce
the membrane of skin,
push the liquid,
hold the needle in for five beats.

Medicine Wheel

Approaching the hospital, she calls in the spirits of the west,
of science and surfaces and accurate measurement.
Early light shredding the sky behind the tower

reminds her of all the dawns to come: false dawns,
divine sparks, hot heads and hot flushes, tempers inflamed
and snap decisions. For these many fires, she calls in

the spirits of the east, takes deep breaths in the car park,
prepares for the piped-about air inside, she calls in
the spirits of the north, the sylphs of oxygen and nitrous oxide,

praying that she might be giddy and feel no pain
as they suck out ten of her moons and add them in a petridish
to that thousand eyed demon, the copious squiggle of spermatozoa.

She chooses a white seat in the waiting room near a potted palm.
Her husband will arrive soon and then it will all begin.
Love Shack is on the radio and she thinks of the room
where he will produce the goods, its clamminess.

Out the window, herb Robert is taking hold and pennywort
has snuck into some wallcracks. Is that three-cornered leek?
She'll pick some once all this is over.

All that remain are the spirits of the south, which are completion
and fruiting and endings, according to her book
on how to be shaman.

So, entering the room, she calls them in too,
and just to be sure, she calls in again the spirits of the west,
of big data and small miracles,
of brisk nurses striding the lino like wolf-women.

The Art

It is only a tiny enhancement of nature
to enter the calcifying dark of a cave
and in the tallow-gloam pick out a dorsal
line of stag, a suggestion of bison,
mammoth prongs, an antelope heel.

It takes a human mind to dream it
and a flicker of ochre. In the right hands,
rock contours transform easily to animal.
The finger nudges and steers the stones,
goads them into yielding their ghosts.

Song of the Day Five Blastocyst

She knows me well, for she has framed
me in her mind before,
hand-drawn my circle,
listed all my suitable names.
She barely dared to think I'd really surface
as a bona-fide working chrysalis
who's snared and snuggled a soul.
Now I knock at her womb door,
ready, willing and trembling.
Gurgling, transfiguring,
becoming whole by testing
the bounds of my being,
I'm poised at life's perimeter,
grow, millimetre by millimetre.

The Thought is the Charm

She pees on a stick
and it says no,
it goes straight in the bin.

She drops a teabag into a cup,
gathers herself into her body
and feels no gurgle there, no glow.

The kettle whistles.
Water knows far better than she,
the moment it leaves one state for another.

How do we all bear to live
in a world where none of us knows
where we really came from?

First thing on Monday,
she promises herself,
she'll research her family tree.

What were all my mothers' names?
The thought is the charm,
because out of view,

on the stick in the bin,
a very pale line appears,
blue and thin.

Scan

A white machine
held to her gelled stomach
crackles with ghost harmonics.

Her insides sound like the sky -
miles-out lines sing like contrails
blending into blue air.

But then they close in on it
and everything shrinks.

Her stomach is a sea-cave
and in it, a tiny drum is banging,
bone on skin

summoning the animal
it is made from,

a new beat pulsing
in – in – in –
at the very centre of her life.

Girl in Aspic

Pickled angel
in the burgundy dark,
wings for legs,
beating arc for a heart,

you subsist
on a sticky intimacy
of sugars and fears,

scrape by on a tinnitus
of fluid-sob and blood-throb.

I'll preserve you in aspic
as long as I can,
my grub, my potted pangolin, my
specimen.

But soon you'll kick
to join with the gleam
of perpetual change.
You'll exceed our purview,

slip out the alleys
of our metropolis,
leave it behind
like a wet home town
you'll never return to.

Belly

Oh squat god,
protector-ogre
of my sealed-in life,

your solemn eyemouth
once sprouted a vine
that attached me
to my mother's insides.

Fat statue in the desert
standing stout,
your button
a single hooded eye,
with a baby for a mind,

I yield to your knowing.

Old skin face,
tell me again
how I am a nothing
in history's deep dream

and how we're all born
from this same African gourd.

Epilogue

Womb

I am looking at a tree.

I regurgitate my tea and the water rushes up into the tap. It's getting earlier and earlier. Soon, we are reversing around the Dordogne as summer flies unpick themselves from the windscreen.

Mum and Dad's ashes turn to flesh in Rotherham crematorium as they go back to exhaling cigarettes and un-watching Crimewatch in a series of bungalows. Meanwhile, at the London Olympics everyone is running backwards. Fewer and fewer people are tapping at computers which are getting slower and slower, as their modems get louder and louder. East London is getting worse. Camden Town is getting better. Canary Wharf is getting lower, Brixton is getting blacker. I go back to university, unmeet my husband, the millennium comes in an implosion of fireworks.

In Berlin, spray paint peels off the wall, liquefies, is sucked into a can. The same thing happens in New York, where everybody is breakdancing. Suddenly, a lot of my friends are getting really small. They are stuffed back, scream-inhaling into the wombs of their scream-inhaling mothers. Somehow, I am still here and hair is being cut longer. The Beatles are back together and all their records are spinning backwards. Except the ones with hidden satanic messages, which are spinning forwards.

Soon, my mother is pushed back into grandma's womb and women everywhere leave factories and start unpicking their knitting. Hemlines get lower and lower and dresses suddenly puff to a sheen as everything gets slower and slower, but there are still wombs. Marie Antoinette finds her head. Men wear wigs, then tights and Columbus or the Vikings lose America. The Mongols and Muslims and Goths and Christians and Romans retreat, retreat, cities disappearing. Cleopatra brushes off her make-up. Wheat fields grass over, ceramics turn to clay, stone circles are dismantled, cave artists brush ochre back onto pallets and it's wombs and wombs all the way until the last few people hop back across the savannah, their arms getting longer and longer.

The trees welcome them back.

LIVE CANON